Success With

Fractions & Decimals

SCHOLASTIC

Editor: Ourania Papacharalambous
Cover design by Tannaz Fassihi; cover illustration by Kevin Zimmer
Interior design by Mina Chen
Interior illustrations by Don O'Connor (8, 10, 14, 18, 22, 32, 36–37, 39, 44); Doug Jones (7, 11–12, 41); Mike Moran (16, 35)
All other images © Shutterstock.com

ISBN 978-1-338-79835-7
Scholastic Inc., 557 Broadway, New York, NY 10012
Copyright © 2022 Scholastic Inc.
All rights reserved. Printed in the U.S.A.
First printing, January 2022
2 3 4 5 6 7 8 9 10   40   29 28 27 26 25 24

INTRODUCTION

Parents and teachers alike will find *Scholastic Success With Fractions & Decimals* to be a valuable resource. Students will enjoy completing a wide variety of engaging activities as they sharpen their skills with fractions and decimals. On page 4, you will find a list of the key skills covered in the activities throughout this book. Remember to praise students for their efforts and successes!

TABLE OF CONTENTS

Grade-Appropriate Skills Covered in *Scholastic Success With Fractions & Decimals: Grade 5*

Read, write, and compare decimals to thousandths.

Read and write decimals to thousandths using base-ten numerals, number names, and expanded form.

Compare two decimals to thousandths based on meanings of the digits in each place, using >, =, and < symbols to record the results of comparisons.

Use place value understanding to round decimals to any place.

Add, subtract, multiply, and divide decimals to hundredths, using concrete models or drawings and strategies based on place value, properties of operations, and/or the relationship between addition and subtraction; relate the strategy to a written method and explain the reasoning used.

Add and subtract fractions with unlike denominators (including mixed numbers) by replacing given fractions with equivalent fractions in such a way as to produce an equivalent sum or difference of fractions with like denominators.

Apply and extend previous understandings of multiplication to multiply a fraction or whole number by a fraction.

Interpret the product $(a/b) \times q$ as a parts of a partition of q into b equal parts; equivalently, as the result of a sequence of operations $a \times q \div b$.

Interpret division of a whole number by a unit fraction, and compute such quotients.

Jumping Lily Pads!

A fraction consists of two parts.

 $\dfrac{5}{}$

The **numerator** tells how many parts are being identified.

 $\dfrac{5}{6} = \dfrac{5}{6}$

The **denominator** tells how many equal parts there are.

Identify the fraction of the shaded part for each shape.

There were 9 lily pads on the pond. On 4 of the lily pads sat a frog. On another sheet of paper, draw a picture to show this fractional set.

Let's Split It Up

To find the fractional part of a number, follow these steps.

$\frac{3}{4}$ of 12 ⟶ $4\overline{)12}$ with $\frac{3}{-12}\overline{0}$

$3 \times 3 = 9$

1. Divide the whole number by the denominator.

2. Multiply the quotient by the numerator.

$\frac{3}{4}$ of 12 = 9

Find the fractional part of each whole number. Shade each box to show the answer.

1 $\frac{1}{3}$ of 9 = ____

$\frac{1}{4}$ of 8 = ____

$\frac{1}{6}$ of 12 = ____

Find the fractional part of each number.

2 $\frac{1}{5}$ of 10 = ____

$\frac{1}{8}$ of 16 = ____

$\frac{3}{5}$ of 15 = ____

3 $\frac{3}{4}$ of 20 = ____

$\frac{5}{6}$ of 30 = ____

$\frac{3}{7}$ of 14 = ____

4 $\frac{6}{8}$ of 32 = ____

$\frac{2}{9}$ of 18 = ____

$\frac{1}{2}$ of 20 = ____

5 $\frac{1}{6}$ of 18 = ____

$\frac{1}{8}$ of 40 = ____

$\frac{1}{7}$ of 21 = ____

You Call That Equal?

Equivalent fractions have the same amount.

$$\frac{3}{4} = \frac{}{8}$$

Equivalent fractions are the same amount of pizza, with simply different size slices!

$$\frac{1 \times 4}{2 \times 4} = \frac{3}{4}$$

What times 2 equals 8? 4! Then, multiply the numerator by 4.

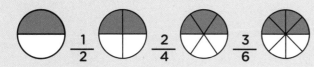 $\frac{1}{2}$ $\frac{2}{4}$ $\frac{3}{6}$ $\frac{4}{8}$

Write the equivalent fractions.

 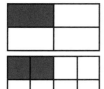

___ = ___   ___ = ___   ___ = ___   ___ = ___

Find each equivalent fraction.

2 $\dfrac{2}{7} = \dfrac{}{21}$ $\qquad$ $\dfrac{3}{6} = \dfrac{}{12}$ $\qquad$ $\dfrac{3}{4} = \dfrac{}{8}$ $\qquad$ $\dfrac{3}{7} = \dfrac{}{14}$

3 $\dfrac{5}{6} = \dfrac{}{36}$ $\qquad$ $\dfrac{5}{8} = \dfrac{}{16}$ $\qquad$ $\dfrac{2}{6} = \dfrac{}{36}$ $\qquad$ $\dfrac{3}{7} = \dfrac{}{49}$

4 $\dfrac{3}{4} = \dfrac{}{16}$ $\qquad$ $\dfrac{7}{9} = \dfrac{}{27}$ $\qquad$ $\dfrac{5}{9} = \dfrac{}{27}$ $\qquad$ $\dfrac{7}{10} = \dfrac{}{100}$

Let's Climb to the Top!

Multiples of a number can be found by multiplying that number by 0, 1, 2, 3, 4, ...
The multiples of 3 are 0, 3, 6, 9, 12, ...

The **least common multiple (LCM)** of two numbers is the least number other than 0 that is a multiple of each. To find the least common multiple of two numbers, find the multiples of each number.

Multiples of 3: 0, 3, 6, 9, 12, 15
Multiples of 4: 0, 4, 8, 12, 16, 20

The first multiple after 0 that is the same is 12. The LCM is 12.

Find the least common multiple for each set of numbers.

4, 7 = ____

3, 6 = ____

2, 5 = ____

3, 5 = ____

2, 3 = ____

4, 5 = ____

5, 6 = ____

2, 4 = ____

2, 7 = ____

3, 7 = ____

4, 6 = ____

4, 8 = ____

2, 8 = ____

3, 8 = ____

5, 7 = ____

5, 8 = ____

2, 10 = ____

4, 12 = ____

2, 9 = ____

6, 8 = ____

4, 9 = ____

5, 10 = ____

3, 9 = ____

6, 7 = ____

3, 4 = ____

8, 10 = ____

4, 10 = ____

Start!

You made it!

Ready to Reduce

A **factor** is a number that divides evenly into another number. The **greatest common factor (GCF)** of two numbers is the greatest number that is a factor of each. To reduce a fraction to lowest terms, follow these steps.

$$\frac{8}{12} \qquad\qquad \frac{8 \div 4}{12 \div 4} = \frac{2}{3} \qquad\qquad \frac{2}{3}$$

1. Find the greatest common factor.
Factors of 8 = 1, 2, 4, 8
Factors of 12 = 1, 2, 3, 4, 6, 12
The GCF = 4

2. Divide the numerator and the denominator by the GCF.

3. Since 2 and 3 have no common factors other than 1, the fraction is in lowest terms.

**Write the factors for each set of numbers below.
Circle the greatest common factor.**

1 Factors of 5: _____

Factors of 15: _____

2 Factors of 6: _____

Factors of 18: _____

3 Factors of 3: _____

Factors of 21: _____

4 Factors of 7: _____

Factors of 28: _____

Find the GCF. Reduce.

1 $\dfrac{4 \div}{10 \div} = $ ____ $\dfrac{6 \div}{12 \div} = $ ____ $\dfrac{3 \div}{12 \div} = $ ____

2 $\dfrac{4 \div}{20 \div} = $ ____ $\dfrac{3 \div}{21 \div} = $ ____ $\dfrac{5 \div}{15 \div} = $ ____

3 $\dfrac{7 \div}{21 \div} = $ ____ $\dfrac{3 \div}{24 \div} = $ ____ $\dfrac{7 \div}{28 \div} = $ ____

It's Time to Reduce

A fraction is in **lowest terms** if the numerator and denominator have no common factors other than 1. To reduce a fraction to lowest terms, follow these steps.

$$\frac{5}{10}$$

1. Find the GCF for 5 and 10.

$$\frac{5 \div 5}{10 \div 5} = \frac{1}{2}$$

2. Divide.

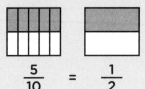

$$\frac{5}{10} = \frac{1}{2}$$

Shade each space with a fraction in lowest terms blue. Shade each space with a fraction not in lowest terms yellow.

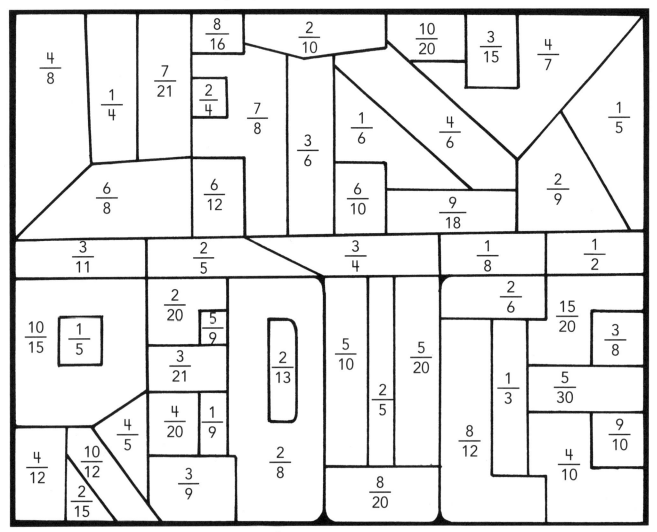

 On another sheet of paper, reduce each fraction that is shaded yellow.

Which Way Did He Go?

To compare fractions, first look at the denominators. If the denominators are different, follow these steps.

$$\frac{2}{3}$$
$$\frac{5}{6}$$

$$\frac{2}{3} = \frac{4}{6}$$
$$\frac{5}{6} = \frac{5}{6}$$

$$\frac{4}{6} < \frac{5}{6}$$

1. Find the LCM for the denominators.

2. Use the LCM to make equivalent fractions with a common denominator.

3. Compare.

Write >, or <, or = to compare each set of fractions.

1 $\frac{1}{2} \bigcirc \frac{3}{4}$ $\frac{5}{6} \bigcirc \frac{10}{12}$ $\frac{3}{8} \bigcirc \frac{1}{16}$ $\frac{3}{10} \bigcirc \frac{4}{5}$

2 $\frac{3}{7} \bigcirc \frac{1}{14}$ $\frac{6}{8} \bigcirc \frac{1}{4}$ $\frac{4}{6} \bigcirc \frac{4}{18}$ $\frac{8}{12} \bigcirc \frac{2}{3}$

3 $\frac{4}{7} \bigcirc \frac{4}{21}$ $\frac{5}{11} \bigcirc \frac{5}{22}$ $\frac{8}{9} \bigcirc \frac{2}{18}$ $\frac{7}{8} \bigcirc \frac{7}{24}$

 Kendall saw 2 deer in the forest. He quietly watched as each ate berries from 2 bushes. When Kendall moved closer, the deer heard him and scampered away. Kendall determined that one deer had eaten 6/8 of the berries on one bush and the other 3/4 of the berries on another bush. Which deer had eaten the most? Show your work on another sheet of paper.

Howling Fun

To change an improper fraction to a mixed number, follow these steps.

$$\frac{13}{6} \qquad 6\overline{)\begin{array}{c}2\\13\\-12\\\hline 1\end{array}}$$

1. Divide the denominator into the numerator.

$$6\overline{)\begin{array}{c}2R1\\13\\-12\\\hline 1\end{array}} = 2\frac{1}{6}$$

2. The remainder becomes the numerator. The divisor becomes the denominator.

$$\frac{12}{6} \qquad 6\overline{)\begin{array}{c}2\\12\\-12\\\hline 0\end{array}}$$

3. If there is no remainder, the improper fraction becomes a whole number.

Change each improper fraction to a mixed or whole number. Then, use the code to answer the question below.

(A) $\frac{18}{7} =$ 　　　　 (H) $\frac{19}{7} =$ 　　　　 (S) $\frac{18}{9} =$

(B) $\frac{28}{7} =$ 　　　　 (I) $\frac{14}{3} =$ 　　　　 (T) $\frac{7}{4} =$

(C) $\frac{19}{5} =$ 　　　　 (K) $\frac{17}{4} =$ 　　　　 (U) $\frac{20}{6} =$

(E) $\frac{15}{4} =$ 　　　　 (R) $\frac{30}{4} =$ 　　　　 (W) $\frac{11}{5} =$

Why did the dog howl?

$$\overline{4} \quad \overline{3\frac{3}{4}} \quad \overline{3\frac{4}{5}} \quad \overline{2\frac{4}{7}} \quad \overline{3\frac{2}{6}} \quad \overline{2} \quad \overline{3\frac{3}{4}}$$

$$\overline{4\frac{2}{3}} \quad \overline{1\frac{3}{4}} \quad \overline{2} \quad \overline{2\frac{4}{7}} \quad \overline{2\frac{1}{5}}$$

$$\overline{1\frac{3}{4}} \quad \overline{2\frac{5}{7}} \quad \overline{3\frac{3}{4}} \quad \overline{1\frac{3}{4}} \quad \overline{7\frac{2}{4}} \quad \overline{3\frac{3}{4}} \quad \overline{3\frac{3}{4}}$$

$$\overline{4} \quad \overline{2\frac{4}{7}} \quad \overline{7\frac{2}{4}} \quad \overline{4\frac{1}{4}}$$

An Ocean of Fun

To change a mixed number to an improper fraction, follow these steps.

$3\frac{1}{5}$ $3 \times 5 = 15$

$15 + 1 = 16$

$3\frac{1}{5} = \frac{16}{5}$

1. Multiply the whole number and denominator.

2. Add the numerator to the product.

3. Place this sum over the denominator.

Change each mixed number to an improper fraction.

$1\frac{4}{7} =$

$1\frac{3}{8} =$

$4\frac{5}{8} =$

$4\frac{3}{5} =$

$5\frac{1}{4} =$

$7\frac{1}{2} =$

$7\frac{1}{4} =$

$6\frac{7}{9} =$

$4\frac{2}{5} =$

$1\frac{3}{4} =$

$7\frac{2}{3} =$

$9\frac{1}{2} =$

$3\frac{2}{7} =$

$4\frac{4}{5} =$

$8\frac{1}{2} =$

$5\frac{1}{5} =$

$2\frac{1}{6} =$

$3\frac{5}{6} =$

$5\frac{7}{8} =$

Yea or Neigh?

To add fractions with the same denominator, follow these steps.

$$\frac{3}{8} + \frac{3}{8} = \frac{6}{}$$

1. Add the numerators.

$$\frac{3}{8} + \frac{3}{8} = \frac{6}{8}$$

2. The denominators remain the same.

$$\frac{6}{8} = \frac{3}{4}$$

3. Reduce to lowest terms.

Add. Then, use the code below to answer the riddle. Reduce to lowest terms.

What's the difference between kids and horses when it comes to voting on whether to have spaghetti for dinner?

$$\frac{3}{7} + \frac{2}{7} \qquad \frac{6}{12} + \frac{3}{12} \qquad \frac{5}{8} + \frac{2}{8} \qquad \frac{2}{4} + \frac{3}{4} \qquad \frac{3}{16} + \frac{4}{16}$$

$$\frac{7}{9} + \frac{1}{9} \qquad \frac{3}{8} + \frac{1}{8} \qquad \frac{7}{12} + \frac{6}{12} \qquad \frac{5}{6} + \frac{2}{6} \qquad \frac{3}{6} + \frac{1}{6}$$

$$\frac{3}{20} + \frac{4}{20} \qquad \frac{6}{5} + \frac{1}{5} \qquad \frac{5}{4} + \frac{3}{4} \qquad \frac{10}{5} + \frac{16}{5} \qquad \frac{5}{8} + \frac{7}{8}$$

$$\frac{4}{9} + \frac{1}{9} \qquad \frac{4}{2} + \frac{4}{2} \qquad \frac{3}{11} + \frac{4}{11}$$

munching	=	$\frac{7}{20}$
crunching	=	2

on	=	$5\frac{1}{5}$	Kids	=	$\frac{5}{7}$	They'd	=	$1\frac{1}{12}$
will	=	$\frac{3}{4}$	be	=	$\frac{2}{3}$	oats	=	$1\frac{1}{2}$
yea	=	$1\frac{1}{4}$	and	=	$\frac{7}{16}$	rather	=	$1\frac{1}{6}$
and	=	$1\frac{2}{5}$	and	=	$\frac{5}{9}$	neigh(nay)!	=	$\frac{1}{2}$

!	=	$\frac{7}{11}$
horses	=	$\frac{8}{9}$
hay	=	4
vote	=	$\frac{7}{8}$

Fraction Tic-Tac-Toe

To add fractions with unlike denominators, follow these steps.

$\dfrac{1}{3} = \dfrac{}{6}$
$+\dfrac{2}{6} = \dfrac{}{6}$

1. Find the common denominator.

$\dfrac{1}{3} = \dfrac{2}{6}$
$\dfrac{2}{6} = \dfrac{2}{6}$

2. Find equivalent fractions.

$\dfrac{2}{6}$
$+\dfrac{2}{6}$
$\dfrac{4}{6}$

3. Add.

$\dfrac{4 \div 2}{6 \div 2} = \dfrac{2}{3}$

4. Reduce to lowest terms.

Add. Reduce to lowest terms. Then, use the Key to fill in the X's and O's.

Key

$\dfrac{3}{5} = $ O	$\dfrac{7}{8} = $ O
$\dfrac{4}{5} = $ O	$\dfrac{1}{4} = $ O
$\dfrac{4}{15} = $ O	$\dfrac{5}{12} = $ X
$\dfrac{4}{9} = $ X	$\dfrac{7}{9} = $ O
$\dfrac{3}{14} = $ X	$\dfrac{1}{2} = $ X
$\dfrac{3}{8} = $ X	$\dfrac{3}{10} = $ X
$\dfrac{2}{3} = $ O	$\dfrac{7}{12} = $ O
$\dfrac{5}{8} = $ O	$\dfrac{5}{6} = $ X
$\dfrac{3}{4} = $ X	$1 = $ O
$\dfrac{7}{16} = $ X	

1

$\dfrac{1}{2}$ $+\dfrac{1}{8}$	$\dfrac{1}{2}$ $+\dfrac{1}{4}$	$\dfrac{1}{6}$ $+\dfrac{1}{2}$
$\dfrac{1}{4}$ $+\dfrac{1}{8}$	$\dfrac{1}{5}$ $+\dfrac{1}{10}$	$\dfrac{1}{3}$ $+\dfrac{1}{6}$
$\dfrac{1}{2}$ $+\dfrac{1}{10}$	$\dfrac{1}{5}$ $+\dfrac{1}{15}$	$\dfrac{1}{3}$ $+\dfrac{1}{9}$

2

$\dfrac{1}{4}$ $+\dfrac{5}{8}$	$\dfrac{1}{6}$ $+\dfrac{1}{12}$	$\dfrac{1}{3}$ $+\dfrac{1}{12}$
$\dfrac{2}{3}$ $+\dfrac{2}{6}$	$\dfrac{1}{2}$ $+\dfrac{1}{12}$	$\dfrac{1}{2}$ $+\dfrac{2}{6}$
$\dfrac{1}{7}$ $+\dfrac{1}{14}$	$\dfrac{3}{16}$ $+\dfrac{1}{4}$	$\dfrac{2}{3}$ $+\dfrac{1}{9}$

Hold On!

Add. Change improper fractions to mixed numbers. Reduce to lowest terms. Then, use the code to answer the riddle below.

O $\dfrac{1}{2}$
$+\dfrac{1}{3}$

W $\dfrac{1}{4}$
$+\dfrac{1}{3}$

E $\dfrac{1}{5}$
$+\dfrac{1}{2}$

G $\dfrac{2}{3}$
$+\dfrac{1}{7}$

S $\dfrac{4}{5}$
$+\dfrac{2}{3}$

A $\dfrac{1}{3}$
$+\dfrac{3}{9}$

L $\dfrac{1}{4}$
$+\dfrac{1}{7}$

O $\dfrac{2}{5}$
$+\dfrac{1}{3}$

I $\dfrac{3}{4}$
$+\dfrac{4}{5}$

N $\dfrac{2}{9}$
$+\dfrac{1}{2}$

R $\dfrac{3}{5}$
$+\dfrac{1}{4}$

D $\dfrac{2}{4}$
$+\dfrac{4}{6}$

H $\dfrac{5}{8}$
$+\dfrac{3}{5}$

! $\dfrac{2}{6}$
$+\dfrac{1}{5}$

U $\dfrac{3}{8}$
$+\dfrac{2}{7}$

N $\dfrac{3}{6}$
$+\dfrac{1}{4}$

Y $\dfrac{3}{7}$
$+\dfrac{1}{4}$

Why was the cowboy a lot of laughs?

___ ___ ___   ___ ___ ___   ___ ___ ___ ___ ___ ___
$1\dfrac{9}{40}$ $\dfrac{7}{10}$ $\dfrac{7}{12}$ $\dfrac{2}{3}$ $1\dfrac{7}{15}$ $\dfrac{2}{3}$ $\dfrac{11}{28}$ $\dfrac{7}{12}$ $\dfrac{2}{3}$ $\dfrac{19}{28}$ $1\dfrac{7}{15}$

___ ___ ___ ___ ___ ___ ___   ___ ___ ___ ___ ___ ___ ___
$1\dfrac{9}{40}$ $\dfrac{5}{6}$ $\dfrac{17}{20}$ $1\dfrac{7}{15}$ $1\dfrac{11}{20}$ $\dfrac{3}{4}$ $\dfrac{17}{21}$ $\dfrac{2}{3}$ $\dfrac{17}{20}$ $\dfrac{11}{15}$ $\dfrac{37}{56}$ $\dfrac{13}{18}$ $1\dfrac{1}{6}$ $\dfrac{8}{15}$

The Rapids Are Approaching!

To add mixed numbers, follow these steps.

$1\frac{2}{4} = \frac{4}{8}$
$+ \quad 1\frac{6}{8} = \frac{6}{8}$

1. Find equivalent fractions.

$1\frac{4}{8}$
$+ \quad 1\frac{6}{8}$
$\frac{10}{8} = 1\frac{2}{8}$

2. Add the fractions. Change the improper fraction to a mixed number.

$\overset{1}{1\frac{4}{8}}$
$+ \quad 1\frac{6}{8}$
$3\frac{2}{8}$

3. Add the whole numbers.

$3\frac{1}{4}$

4. Reduce the fraction to lowest terms.

Add. Reduce to lowest terms.

1.
$1\frac{1}{2}$
$+ \; 3\frac{1}{8}$

$4\frac{1}{2}$
$+ \; 2\frac{4}{6}$

$3\frac{1}{2}$
$+ \; 1\frac{3}{4}$

2.
$2\frac{3}{7}$
$+ \; 1\frac{1}{14}$

$3\frac{1}{6}$
$+ \quad \frac{1}{2}$

$1\frac{1}{2}$
$+ \; 2\frac{1}{3}$

3.
$4\frac{2}{3}$
$+ \; 3\frac{1}{6}$

$3\frac{5}{8}$
$+ \; 1\frac{4}{8}$

$4\frac{1}{6}$
$+ \; 1\frac{1}{2}$

$5\frac{3}{9}$
$+ \; 1\frac{1}{3}$

4.
$2\frac{3}{5}$
$+ \; 1\frac{1}{4}$

$3\frac{1}{3}$
$+ \quad \frac{4}{9}$

$6\frac{1}{2}$
$+ \; 2\frac{4}{6}$

$1\frac{1}{4}$
$+ \; 3\frac{7}{8}$

A Grand Canyon

To subtract fractions with unlike denominators, follow these steps.

$$\frac{3}{4} = \frac{}{8}$$
$$-\ \frac{4}{8} = \frac{}{8}$$

1. Find the least common denominator.

$$\frac{3 \times 2}{4 \times 2} = \frac{6}{8}$$
$$-\ \frac{4}{8}$$

2. Find equivalent fractions.

$$\frac{6}{8}$$
$$-\ \frac{4}{8}$$
$$\frac{2}{8}$$

3. Subtract.

$$\frac{2}{8} = \frac{1}{4}$$

4. Reduce to lowest terms.

Subtract. Reduce to lowest terms. Then, write the numerator of the difference from the problems listed below to complete the interesting fact.

A $\frac{7}{14} - \frac{3}{7}$

B $\frac{4}{5} - \frac{10}{15}$

C $\frac{4}{6} - \frac{5}{12}$

D $\frac{2}{3} - \frac{1}{12}$

E $\frac{4}{7} - \frac{7}{14}$

F $\frac{23}{25} - \frac{3}{5}$

G $\frac{4}{8} - \frac{4}{16}$

H $\frac{7}{10} - \frac{3}{5}$

I $\frac{2}{3} - \frac{4}{9}$

J $\frac{5}{6} - \frac{3}{12}$

K $\frac{3}{4} - \frac{8}{12}$

L $\frac{9}{10} - \frac{3}{5}$

M $\frac{4}{7} - \frac{3}{14}$

N $\frac{7}{9} - \frac{3}{18}$

O $\frac{4}{5} - \frac{6}{15}$

Grand Canyon National Park covers

_____ , _____ _____ _____ , _____ _____ _____ acres.
   K   I   C   F   L   D   M

Sailing Through Subtraction

Subtract. Reduce to lowest terms.

1
$\frac{4}{5}$ $- \frac{1}{2}$

$\frac{7}{8}$ $- \frac{2}{3}$

$\frac{1}{2}$ $- \frac{1}{3}$

$\frac{1}{3}$ $- \frac{1}{4}$

2
$\frac{3}{6}$ $- \frac{1}{5}$

$\frac{4}{5}$ $- \frac{1}{3}$

$\frac{6}{8}$ $- \frac{1}{3}$

$\frac{3}{4}$ $- \frac{1}{5}$

3
$\frac{6}{7}$ $- \frac{1}{4}$

$\frac{4}{5}$ $- \frac{1}{6}$

$\frac{1}{2}$ $- \frac{1}{9}$

$\frac{2}{3}$ $- \frac{1}{2}$

4
$\frac{3}{7}$ $- \frac{2}{5}$

$\frac{4}{7}$ $- \frac{1}{2}$

$\frac{7}{8}$ $- \frac{1}{3}$

$\frac{2}{3}$ $- \frac{2}{5}$

5
$\frac{5}{8}$ $- \frac{1}{5}$

$\frac{2}{3}$ $- \frac{1}{7}$

$\frac{8}{9}$ $- \frac{1}{2}$

$\frac{4}{5}$ $- \frac{2}{3}$

Sliding Through Subtraction

To subtract mixed numbers, follow these steps.

$3\frac{2}{3} = \frac{8}{12}$

$-\ 2\frac{2}{4} = \frac{6}{12}$

1. Find the least common denominator. Then, find equivalent fractions.

$3\frac{8}{12}$

$-\ 2\frac{6}{12}$

_____

$\frac{2}{12}$

2. Subtract the fractions.

$3\frac{8}{12}$

$-\ 2\frac{6}{12}$

_____

$1\frac{2}{12} = 1\frac{1}{6}$

3. Subtract the whole numbers. Reduce to lowest terms.

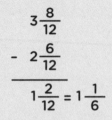

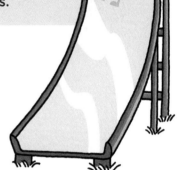

Subtract. Reduce to lowest terms.

1

$6\frac{3}{5}$ $-\ 3\frac{1}{5}$

$4\frac{6}{7}$ $-\ 3\frac{5}{7}$

$5\frac{4}{5}$ $-\ 3\frac{3}{5}$

2

$7\frac{5}{9}$ $-\ 3\frac{2}{9}$

$8\frac{3}{4}$ $-\ 4\frac{1}{4}$

$5\frac{7}{8}$ $-\ 3\frac{5}{8}$

$9\frac{9}{10}$ $-\ 6\frac{6}{10}$

$4\frac{7}{11}$ $-\ 3\frac{4}{11}$

3

$5\frac{2}{3}$ $-\ 2\frac{1}{6}$

$5\frac{3}{5}$ $-\ 2\frac{1}{10}$

$6\frac{3}{4}$ $-\ 2\frac{2}{4}$

$8\frac{4}{7}$ $-\ 3\frac{2}{14}$

$4\frac{7}{8}$ $-\ 2\frac{6}{8}$

4

$8\frac{3}{4}$ $-\ 2\frac{1}{6}$

$9\frac{3}{4}$ $-\ 3\frac{6}{12}$

$6\frac{4}{9}$ $-\ 2\frac{1}{3}$

$8\frac{1}{3}$ $-\ 3\frac{1}{4}$

$4\frac{1}{6}$ $-\ 2\frac{1}{12}$

A Great Way to Borrow

When borrowing is necessary to subtract fractions, follow these steps.

$$5\frac{2}{5} = 4\frac{5}{5} + \frac{2}{5}$$
$$-\ 3\frac{3}{5}$$

$$4\frac{7}{5}$$
$$-\ 3\frac{3}{5}$$

$$4\frac{7}{5}$$
$$-\ 3\frac{3}{5}$$
$$\frac{4}{5}$$

$$4\frac{7}{5}$$
$$-\ 3\frac{3}{5}$$
$$1\frac{4}{5}$$

1. Borrow 1 from the whole number 5. Change 1 into the fraction 5/5.

2. Add 4 5/5 + 2/5.

3. Subtract the fractions.

4. Subtract the whole numbers. If necessary, reduce to lowest terms.

Add. Reduce to lowest terms. Then, use the code below to answer the question.

Why is borrowing a good thing in math?

| at = $6\frac{3}{4}$ |
| of = $1\frac{3}{7}$ |
| the = $1\frac{1}{2}$ |
| end = $\frac{7}{9}$ |
| you = $2\frac{1}{2}$ |
| don't = $1\frac{3}{5}$ |
| owe = $6\frac{2}{3}$ |
| Because = $1\frac{5}{6}$ |
| anything = $2\frac{3}{4}$ |
| back = $1\frac{3}{4}$ |
| problem = $5\frac{8}{11}$ |

_____   _____   _____   _____

$$3\frac{2}{6}$$ $$5\frac{1}{4}$$ $$4\frac{2}{5}$$ $$8\frac{1}{3}$$
$$-\ 1\frac{3}{6}$$ $$-\ 2\frac{3}{4}$$ $$-\ 2\frac{4}{5}$$ $$-\ 1\frac{2}{3}$$

_____   _____   _____   _____

$$6\frac{1}{8}$$ $$6\frac{2}{4}$$ $$6\frac{1}{8}$$ $$2\frac{1}{9}$$
$$-\ 3\frac{4}{8}$$ $$-\ 4\frac{3}{4}$$ $$-\ 4\frac{5}{8}$$ $$-\ 1\frac{3}{9}$$

_____   _____   _____ !

$$3\frac{1}{7}$$ $$4\frac{1}{6}$$ $$9\frac{1}{11}$$
$$-\ 1\frac{5}{7}$$ $$-\ 2\frac{4}{6}$$ $$-\ 3\frac{4}{11}$$

Math Meteors

To subtract fractions and mixed numbers from whole numbers, follow these steps.

$$5 = 4\frac{3}{3}$$
$$-\ 2\frac{1}{3}$$

$$4\frac{3}{3}$$
$$-\ 2\frac{1}{3}$$
$$\frac{2}{3}$$

$$4\frac{3}{3}$$
$$-\ 2\frac{1}{3}$$
$$2\frac{2}{3}$$

1. Change the whole number into a mixed number using the denominator of the fraction.

2. Subtract the fractions.

3. Subtract the whole numbers. If necessary, reduce to lowest terms.

Subtract. Reduce to lowest terms. Then, use the code to learn about a famous meteorite.

E 6
$-\ \frac{4}{8}$

I 5
$-\ 2\frac{1}{2}$

T 3
$-\ 1\frac{2}{5}$

A 6
$-\ \frac{3}{7}$

L 9
$-\ 6\frac{1}{4}$

W 3
$-\ 1\frac{1}{3}$

E 7
$-\ 2\frac{1}{5}$

L 5
$-\ 1\frac{3}{5}$

T 7
$-\ 2\frac{1}{3}$

C 4
$-\ 2\frac{3}{5}$

N 2
$-\ \frac{3}{7}$

G 6
$-\ 3\frac{1}{5}$

S 4
$-\ \frac{3}{7}$

M 9
$-\ 3\frac{1}{6}$

J 8
$-\ \frac{3}{7}$

The largest meteorite found in the United States is called the

_____ _____ _____ _____ _____ _____ _____ _____ _____ **meteorite.**

$1\frac{2}{3}$ $2\frac{1}{2}$ $3\frac{2}{5}$ $2\frac{3}{4}$ $5\frac{4}{7}$ $5\frac{5}{6}$ $4\frac{4}{5}$ $1\frac{3}{5}$ $4\frac{2}{3}$ $5\frac{1}{2}$

Mighty Multiplication

To multiply a whole number and a fraction, follow these steps.

$2 \times \dfrac{3}{4}$ $\dfrac{2}{1} \times \dfrac{3}{4}$ $\dfrac{2 \times 3}{1 \times 4} = \dfrac{6}{4}$ $1\dfrac{2}{4} = 1\dfrac{1}{2}$

1. Change the whole number into a fraction.

2. Multiply the numerators and the denominators.

3. Change the improper fraction to a mixed number. Reduce to lowest terms.

$7 \times \dfrac{1}{8}$

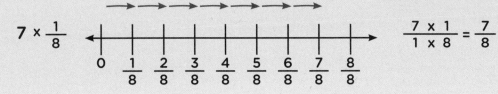

$\dfrac{7 \times 1}{1 \times 8} = \dfrac{7}{8}$

Multiply. Reduce to lowest terms.

1 $3 \times \dfrac{2}{5} =$ $6 \times \dfrac{1}{3} =$ $7 \times \dfrac{1}{4} =$ $5 \times \dfrac{2}{3} =$

2 $4 \times \dfrac{1}{2} =$ $4 \times \dfrac{1}{8} =$ $6 \times \dfrac{2}{3} =$ $6 \times \dfrac{4}{8} =$

3 $5 \times \dfrac{3}{4} =$ $5 \times \dfrac{1}{6} =$ $8 \times \dfrac{1}{4} =$ $9 \times \dfrac{2}{3} =$

4 $7 \times \dfrac{3}{5} =$ $9 \times \dfrac{1}{3} =$ $3 \times \dfrac{2}{4} =$ $4 \times \dfrac{5}{6} =$

5 $7 \times \dfrac{2}{3} =$ $2 \times \dfrac{1}{3} =$ $9 \times \dfrac{1}{2} =$ $7 \times \dfrac{2}{8} =$

Muscular Marvin tried to lift 8 heavy boxes. They were too heavy. He then tried to lift 3/4 of the boxes. He succeeded! How many boxes did he lift? Show your work on another sheet of paper.

It's Raining Multiplication

To multiply fractions, multiply the numerators. Then, multiply the denominators. Reduce to lowest terms.

  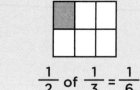

$$\frac{1 \times 1}{2 \times 3} = \frac{1}{6}$$

$\frac{1}{2}$ of $\frac{1}{3}$ $\frac{1}{2}$ of $\frac{1}{3} = \frac{1}{6}$

Multiply. Reduce to lowest terms.

1 $\frac{1}{3} \times \frac{2}{6} =$ $\frac{3}{5} \times \frac{2}{3} =$ $\frac{3}{4} \times \frac{1}{2} =$ $\frac{1}{4} \times \frac{1}{3} =$

2 $\frac{1}{5} \times \frac{1}{6} =$ $\frac{2}{4} \times \frac{1}{2} =$ $\frac{1}{4} \times \frac{2}{3} =$ $\frac{3}{4} \times \frac{1}{3} =$

3 $\frac{4}{8} \times \frac{1}{2} =$ $\frac{1}{8} \times \frac{1}{2} =$ $\frac{1}{5} \times \frac{1}{10} =$ $\frac{1}{3} \times \frac{1}{6} =$

4 $\frac{3}{5} \times \frac{1}{3} =$ $\frac{2}{6} \times \frac{1}{4} =$ $\frac{1}{3} \times \frac{1}{2} =$ $\frac{5}{8} \times \frac{2}{3} =$

5 $\frac{3}{7} \times \frac{3}{6} =$ $\frac{1}{5} \times \frac{1}{4} =$ $\frac{1}{2} \times \frac{1}{4} =$ $\frac{2}{3} \times \frac{3}{4} =$

6 $\frac{3}{5} \times \frac{1}{2} =$ $\frac{4}{6} \times \frac{2}{3} =$ $\frac{1}{2} \times \frac{1}{9} =$ $\frac{3}{4} \times \frac{2}{7} =$

Crazy Word Combos

To multiply fractions and mixed numbers, follow these steps.

$$\frac{1}{3} \times 3\frac{1}{4} \qquad 3\frac{1}{4} = \frac{13}{4} \qquad \frac{1}{3} \times \frac{13}{4} = \frac{13}{12} \qquad \frac{13}{12} = 1\frac{1}{12}$$

1. Change the mixed number into an improper fraction.

2. Multiply.

3. Change the improper fraction to a mixed number. Reduce to lowest terms.

Multiply. If the product can be reduced to a whole number or a fraction, unscramble the crazy word combo. Use the Word Bank below to help you. If the product is a mixed number, disregard.

1

$\frac{2}{3} \times 4\frac{1}{2} =$

d c n o a w h

_____

$\frac{6}{7} \times 1\frac{1}{2} =$

h n f l u s e

_____

$\frac{1}{5} \times 6\frac{1}{2} =$

a d x a l x

_____

2

$\frac{1}{5} \times 3\frac{1}{2} =$

m b r o o o w k

_____

$\frac{4}{5} \times 2\frac{1}{2} =$

k b l o a a w d r

_____

$\frac{3}{5} \times 2\frac{1}{3} =$

a q u r s t l

_____

3

$\frac{1}{2} \times 3\frac{1}{4} =$

m r a u s t u

_____

$\frac{1}{6} \times 1\frac{1}{2} =$

y h l o f u e s

_____

$\frac{6}{7} \times 1\frac{1}{3} =$

a l m n o o z e

_____

4

$\frac{3}{5} \times 3\frac{1}{3} =$

l t i o a e n

_____

$\frac{3}{6} \times 1\frac{1}{3} =$

l c o a o r p

_____

$\frac{1}{5} \times 1\frac{1}{3} =$

b w o c y o

_____

Word Bank

foxglove cowhand toenail housefly cowboy carpool boardwalk bookworm

Division Stars

To divide a whole number by a fraction, follow these steps.

$$4 \div \frac{1}{3} = \qquad 4 = \frac{4}{1} \qquad \frac{1}{3} = \frac{3}{1} \qquad \frac{4 \times 3}{1 \times 1} = \frac{12}{1} \qquad \frac{12}{1} = 12$$

1. Change the whole number into a fraction.

2. Invert $\frac{1}{3}$.

3. Multiply.

4. Change the improper fraction to a mixed number. Reduce to lowest terms.

$$4 \div \frac{1}{3} = 12$$

12 thirds

Divide each of the 4 rectangles into thirds. Total thirds: 12

Divide. Then, write the ones digit in each star in order on the lines below to learn about our star, the sun.

1 $\quad 7 \div \frac{1}{3} =$ $\qquad 7 \div \frac{1}{2} =$ $\qquad 4 \div \frac{1}{2} =$ $\quad 8 \div \frac{1}{4} =$ $\qquad 6 \div \frac{1}{2} =$

2 $\quad 3 \div \frac{1}{5} =$ $\qquad 3 \div \frac{1}{3} =$ $\qquad 9 \div \frac{1}{3} =$ $\qquad 2 \div \frac{1}{3} =$ $\quad 2 \div \frac{1}{4} =$

3 $\quad 5 \div \frac{1}{3} =$ $\quad 3 \div \frac{1}{2} =$ $\qquad 1 \div \frac{1}{2} =$ $\qquad 5 \div \frac{1}{6} =$ $\quad 4 \div \frac{1}{3} =$

4 $\quad 8 \div \frac{1}{2} =$ $\qquad 6 \div \frac{1}{3} =$ $\qquad 5 \div \frac{1}{2} =$ $\quad 5 \div \frac{1}{4} =$ $\quad 3 \div \frac{1}{4} =$

The diameter of the sun is ___ ___ ___ , ___ ___ ___ **miles.**

The Great Divide

To change a fraction to a decimal, follow these steps.

$\frac{4}{10}$ $10\overline{)4}$

1. Divide the numerator by the denominator.

$10\overline{)4}$ 0

2. Divide. Subtract. Add a decimal point and a zero. Divide.

0.4
$10\overline{)4.0}$

0.4
$10\overline{)4.0}$
$\underline{-4\,0}$
0

3. Subtract.

$\frac{4}{10} = 0.4$

Change each fraction to a decimal.

1 $\frac{1}{5} =$ $\frac{3}{6} =$ $\frac{4}{5} =$ $\frac{2}{5} =$

2 $\frac{3}{4} =$ $\frac{3}{8} =$ $\frac{6}{10} =$ $\frac{7}{8} =$

3 $\frac{5}{25} =$ $\frac{1}{4} =$ $\frac{3}{10} =$ $\frac{5}{20} =$

4 $\frac{3}{25} =$ $\frac{4}{8} =$ $\frac{7}{20} =$ $\frac{9}{25} =$

5 $\frac{7}{10} =$ $\frac{5}{8} =$ $\frac{9}{10} =$ $\frac{3}{5} =$

What's the Word?

From the right of the decimal point, decimals are read as tenths, hundredths, and thousandths.

thousands	hundreds	tens	ones		tenths	hundredths	thousandths
4	2	8	6	●	3	1	5

$$\frac{4,286}{\text{Whole number}} \bullet \frac{315}{\text{Fraction of a number}}$$

4,286 ones ● 315 thousandths

Draw a line from each decimal to its word name.

five and three thousandths

four and one hundredth

three hundred forty-two and one tenth

three and twelve hundredths

thirteen and four hundredths

3.12

6.1

56.4

three hundred two thousandths

5.31

4.01

13.04

5.003

sixty-one and four hundredths

0.302

8.3

fifty-six and four tenths

eight and forty-one thousandths

61.04

3.22

five and thirty-one hundredths

5.214

1.002

six and one tenth

8.041

981.42

342.1

eight and three tenths

one and two thousandths

three and twenty-two hundredths

five and two hundred fourteen thousandths

nine hundred eighty-one and forty-two hundredths

What Does Polly Want?

Write a decimal for each diagram. Match each decimal diagram with a word in the Decimal Key below to find out what Polly wants.

> The first digit to the right of the decimal point is the **tenths** place.

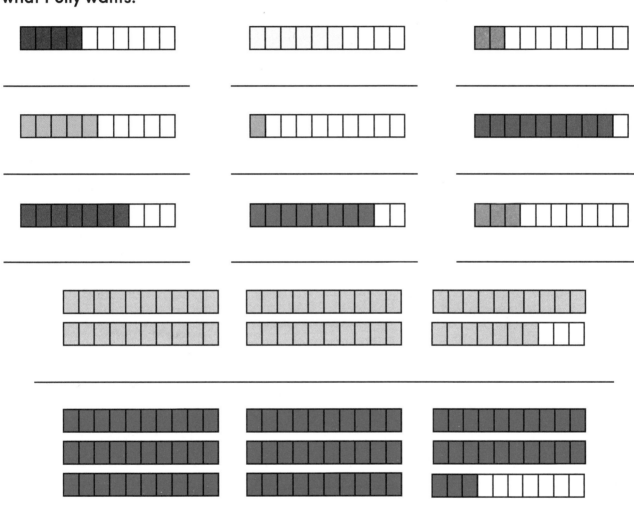

Decimal Key

only = 0.6	tenth = 0.1	cracker = 0.8	that = 0.7	one = 0.5	I = 0.4
your = 5.7	in = 0.3	hand! = 8.3	want = 0.2	of = 0.9	

Sarah's pet parrot Chatter nibbled 2.3 crackers. On another sheet of paper, draw a diagram to show how many crackers Chatter nibbled.

Let's Go Digital!

The second digit to the right of the decimal is the **hundredths** place.

There are 43 hundredths (0.43) shaded in this diagram. That is 43 of the 100 squares available.

Decimal: 0.43

Fraction: $\frac{43}{100}$

ones		tenths	hundredths
0	●	4	3

It is read forty-three hundredths.

Write the decimal for each number word in the Decimal Digital Boxes.

1. three and fifty-four hundredths _____

2. fifty-six and seventy-two hundredths _____

3. ninety-eight hundredths _____

4. twenty-four and two hundredths _____

5. three hundred four and three hundredths _____

6. seventy-five and thirteen hundredths _____

7. eight hundred forty-three and six hundredths _____

8. eighty-nine and twenty-two hundredths _____

9. one hundred thirty-one and seventy-one hundredths _____

10. sixty-nine hundredths _____

11. fifty-two and thirty-two hundredths _____

12. four hundred and fifty-seven hundredths _____

13. twenty-seven and four hundredths _____

14. forty-eight and three hundredths _____

15. fourteen and sixty-two hundredths _____

16. seven hundred eighty-six and two hundredths _____

17. four hundred forty-five and sixty-four hundredths _____

18. six hundred twenty-five and fifty-four hundredths _____

19. nine hundred twenty-eight and twenty-four hundredths _____

20. four and nine tenths _____

Put on Your Thinking Cap

The third digit to the right of the decimal is the **thousandths** place.

thousands	hundreds	tens	ones		tenths	hundredths	thousandths
3	2	3	6	●	3	1	5

	ones		tenths	hundredths	thousandths
	1	●	3	2	4

These decimals are read as follows:

three thousand two hundred thirty-six and four thousandths

one and three hundred twenty-four thousandths

Use the clues to find each missing number.

1 This number has a 9 in the thousandths place and a 1 in the ones place. The total sum of the digits is 17. There are no 3s or 5s and all the digits are greater than 0. The lesser digit is in the tenths place.

_____ . _____ _____ _____

2 Get ready for a tough one! All the digits are different odd numbers between 0 and 10. The number with the greatest value is in the thousands place. The number with the least value is in the tenths place. The remaining numbers are in numerical order beginning in the hundreds place.

_____ , _____ _____ _____ . _____

3 Think hard! There is a 3 in the tens place, a 6 in the thousandths place, and nothing in between except for 2 ones.

_____ _____ . _____ _____ _____

4 Are you up for a challenge? This decimal has a 7 to the left of the decimal point. The sum of the three digits to the right of the decimal point is 15. The greatest of these three digits is one more than 7 and is in the hundredths place. The digit in the tenths place is less than the digit in the thousandths place and is greater than 2.

_____ . _____ _____ _____

5 A real challenge! The two digits to the left of the decimal point are different numbers and their sum is 10. They do not include a 1, 3, or 8. The number with the least value is in the tens place. To the right of the decimal point, the sum of the three digits also totals 10. Two of the digits are the same. The digit in the thousandths place is different than the digits in the tenths and hundredths places and is the same as the digit in the tens place.

_____ _____ . _____ _____ _____

Cross-Decimal Fun

Write the number word for each decimal. Use hyphens when necessary.

Across

1. 0.6   **7.** 0.02
3. 0.08   **8.** 0.09
4. 0.054   **10.** 0.05
5. 0.5   **11.** 0.32
6. 0.3   **12.** 0.026

Down

1. 0.007
2. 0.06
4. 0.4
9. 0.2

A Weighty Decision

A number line can be used to compare decimals.

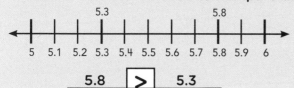

| 5.8 | > | 5.3 |

Eight tenths (5.8) is greater than three tenths (5.3).
Moving to the right on a number line increases the value of a decimal.

| 2.57 | < | 2.75 |

Fifty-seven hundredths (2.57) is less than seventy-five hundredths (2.75).
Moving to the left on a number line decreases the value of a decimal.

Write >, <, or = to compare the decimals.

1   3.4 ☐ 3.5   6.4 ☐ 4.6   5.7 ☐ 5.8   0.1 ☐ 1.01

2   0.8 ☐ 0.1   0.1 ☐ 0.10   0.5 ☐ 0.05   2.41 ☐ 24.1

3   7.4 ☐ 7.40   0.41 ☐ 0.4   3.2 ☐ 0.32   6.41 ☐ 6.41

4   0.7 ☐ 0.07   8.4 ☐ 78.4   6.1 ☐ 6.18

5   5.1 ☐ 0.05   2.9 ☐ 9.2

6   0.3 ☐ 3.03   6.8 ☐ 6.40

7   2.48 ☐ 24.8   0.4 ☐ 0.6

That's an Order!

To put decimals in order from least to greatest, compare digits in the same places.

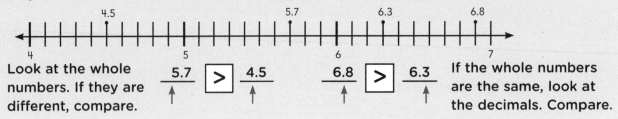

Look at the whole numbers. If they are different, compare.

5.7 > 4.5 6.8 > 6.3

If the whole numbers are the same, look at the decimals. Compare.

Order each set of decimals from least to greatest. Then, write the letters in the same order to spell a math term in the last column.

1 H 4.9   A 4.4   T 4.8   M 4.2   4.2 4.4 4.8 4.9   MATH

2 D 7.7   O 7.3   E 7.9   M 7.0   ___ ___ ___ ___   _____

3 D 0.8   I 0.5   R 0.3   G 0.2   ___ ___ ___ ___   _____

4 R 3.6   A 8.4   E 5.7   A 1.9   ___ ___ ___ ___   _____

5 B 2.89   E 2.98   U 2.47   C 2.16   ___ ___ ___ ___   _____

6 E 8.42   F 0.59   C 6.48   A 3.93   ___ ___ ___ ___   _____

7 E 4.09   A 6.409   M 0.409   N 6.904   ___ ___ ___ ___   _____

8 N 4.06   I 3.92   L 0.92   E 6.9   ___ ___ ___ ___   _____

9 H 9.08   N 4.84   C 5.45   I 1.8   ___ ___ ___ ___   _____

10 P 1.842   I 1.824   F 1.248   L 1.482   ___ ___ ___ ___   _____

11 M 9.05   E 5.09   T 0.59   R 9.005   ___ ___ ___ ___   _____

The Big Roundup (or Down!)

When rounding, if the number is 5 or more, round up. If the number is 4 or less, round down.

3.<u>6</u> = 4

8.<u>4</u> = 8

6.3<u>4</u> = 6.3

9.6<u>6</u> = 9.7

When rounding to the nearest whole number, look at the tenths digit.

When rounding to the nearest tenth, look at the hundredths digit.

Write each decimal and the rounded number in the correct box.

1 Round to the nearest whole number.

4 or less, round down!	5 or more, round up!
2.2 = 2	

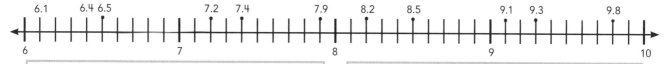

4 or less, round down!	5 or more, round up!

2 Round to the nearest tenth.

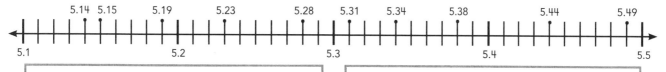

4 or less, round down!	5 or more, round up!

4 or less, round down!	5 or more, round up!

Let's Get Rolling!

Round the decimals on each rock to the nearest hundredths place.
Then, write the rounded decimals in order from least to greatest.

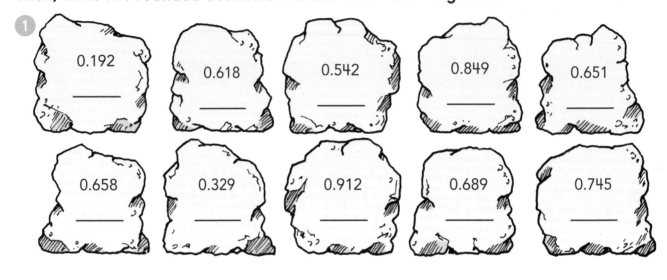

1. 0.192 _____   0.618 _____   0.542 _____   0.849 _____   0.651 _____

   0.658 _____   0.329 _____   0.912 _____   0.689 _____   0.745 _____

_____ _____ _____ _____ _____

_____ _____ _____ _____ _____

2. 6.416 _____   5.914 _____   4.255 _____   3.692 _____   5.346 _____

   4.182 _____   3.145 _____   6.545 _____   7.312 _____   9.425 _____

_____ _____ _____ _____ _____

_____ _____ _____ _____ _____

On another sheet of paper, write three decimals that could be rounded to 5.7 and three decimals that could be rounded to 2.64.

Pile Them Up!

When adding decimals, follow these steps.

```
       1                 1 1              1 1 1            1 1 1
   36.46             36.46             36.46             36.46
 + 13.84           + 13.84           + 13.84           + 13.84
 ─────────         ─────────         ─────────         ─────────
    .  0               .30             0.30             50.30
```

1. Line up the decimal points. Add the hundredths. Regroup.

2. Add the tenths. Regroup.

3. Add the ones. Regroup.

4. Add the tens.

Choose two addends from the decimal pile to make each sum.

1

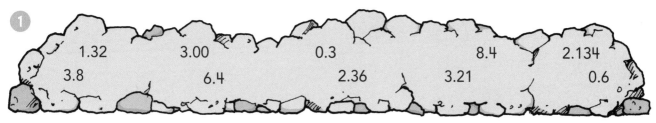

1.32   3.00   0.3   8.4   2.134
3.8   6.4   2.36   3.21   0.6

```
  +            +            +             +             +
─────        ─────       ──────        ──────        ───────
 5.36         0.9         10.2          4.53          10.534
```

2

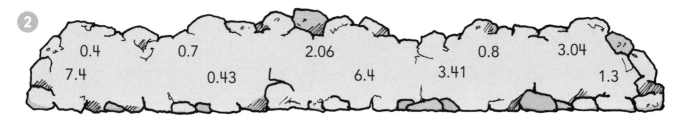

0.4   0.7   2.06   0.8   3.04
7.4   0.43   6.4   3.41   1.3

```
  +            +            +             +             +
─────        ─────       ─────        ──────        ─────
 5.10         1.2         8.1          3.84          7.7
```

3

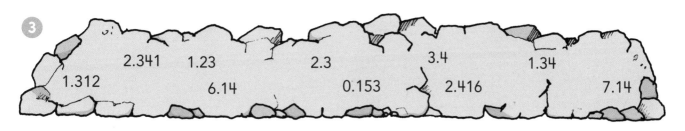

2.341   1.23   2.3   3.4   1.34
1.312   6.14   0.153 2.416   7.14

```
  +            +            +             +             +
─────        ─────       ───────       ──────        ───────
 5.7          7.37        2.494         8.48          3.728
```

Geometric Code Crackers

Use the Shape Bank to write each problem. Add.

Shape Bank

△	= 3.214
▢	= 21.04
◇	= 1.048
○	= 34.218
◺	= 7.06
⬡	= 23.142
⯃	= 0.343
▭	= 6.2
◊	= 0.246
▱	= 1.003
⬠	= 2.14
◈◈◈	= 13.102
◬	= 0.243
⬛	= 8.141
⬭	= 0.203
☆	= 26.31

1. cylinder / rectangle / right-triangle + _____

rhombus / circle / triangle + _____

trapezoid / pentagon / star + _____

2. square / triangle-grid / diamond + _____

octagon / right-triangle / cube + _____

square / rhombus / diamond + _____

3. three-diamonds / circle / right-triangle + _____

octagon / diamond / trapezoid + _____

square / cylinder / star + _____

4. circle / trapezoid / pentagon + _____

cube / diamond + _____

rhombus / triangle / cylinder + _____

5. triangle-grid / square / right-triangle + _____

three-diamonds / circle / rectangle + _____

hexagon / square / triangle + _____

6. star / circle / right-triangle + _____

hexagon / rhombus / cube + _____

diamond / square / triangle + _____

rhombus / octagon / pentagon + _____

Let's Get Going!

To subtract decimals, follow these steps.

8.23 – 1.345 .	8.2$\overset{2\ 1}{3}$0 – 1.345 . 5	8.$\overset{1\ 12\ 1}{2}$$\overset{}{3}$0 – 1.345 . 85	$\overset{7\ 11\ 12\ 1}{8}$.2$\overset{}{3}$0 – 1.345 .885	$\overset{7\ 11\ 12\ 1}{8}$.2$\overset{}{3}$0 – 1.345 6.885
1. Line up the decimal points. Place the decimal point in the answer.	**2.** Add a zero so each decimal has the same number of digits. Borrow. Regroup. Subtract the thousandths.	**3.** Borrow. Regroup. Subtract the hundredths.	**4.** Borrow. Regroup. Subtract the tenths.	**5.** Subtract the ones.

Subtract.

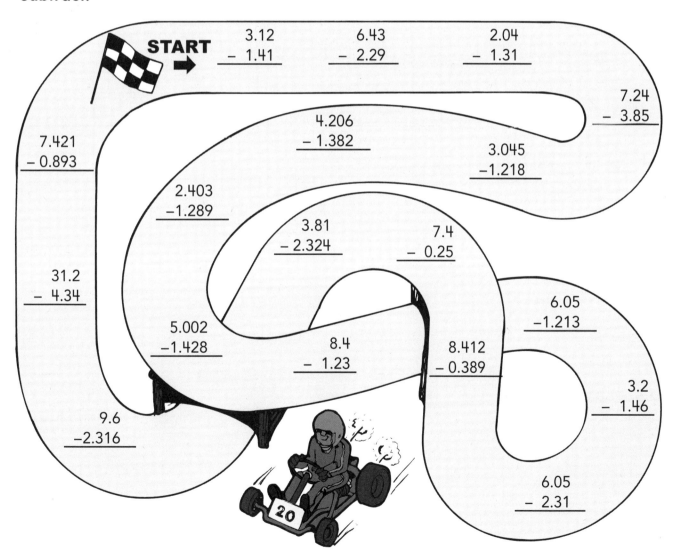

START →

3.12 – 1.41	6.43 – 2.29	2.04 – 1.31

7.24
– 3.85

4.206
– 1.382

7.421
– 0.893

3.045
–1.218

2.403
–1.289

3.81
– 2.324

7.4
– 0.25

31.2
– 4.34

6.05
–1.213

5.002
–1.428

8.4
– 1.23

8.412
– 0.389

3.2
– 1.46

9.6
–2.316

6.05
– 2.31

20

Cross-Decimal Subtraction

To subtract a decimal from
a whole number, add a zero
for each decimal place.
Subtract.

$$\begin{array}{r} 3 \\ -\ 0.246 \end{array}$$

$$\begin{array}{r} {}^{2}\cancel{3}.{}^{9}\cancel{0}{}^{9}\cancel{0}{}^{1}0 \\ -\ 0.246 \\ \hline 2.754 \end{array}$$

Subtract. Decimal points count as a space.

Across

4.
$$\begin{array}{r} 8 \\ -\ 5.002 \end{array}$$

5.
$$\begin{array}{r} 2 \\ -\ 0.982 \end{array}$$

6.
$$\begin{array}{r} 4 \\ -\ 2.467 \end{array}$$

7.
$$\begin{array}{r} 3 \\ -\ 2.403 \end{array}$$

8.
$$\begin{array}{r} 5 \\ -\ 2.48 \end{array}$$

Down

9.
$$\begin{array}{r} 13 \\ -\ 2.89 \end{array}$$

11.
$$\begin{array}{r} 9 \\ -\ 3.546 \end{array}$$

1.
$$\begin{array}{r} 4 \\ -\ 2.006 \end{array}$$

2.
$$\begin{array}{r} 6 \\ -\ 3.419 \end{array}$$

3.
$$\begin{array}{r} 5 \\ -\ 3.891 \end{array}$$

4.
$$\begin{array}{r} 5 \\ -\ 2.642 \end{array}$$

14.
$$\begin{array}{r} 7 \\ -\ 3.002 \end{array}$$

15.
$$\begin{array}{r} 12 \\ -\ 2.412 \end{array}$$

6.
$$\begin{array}{r} 2 \\ -\ 0.48 \end{array}$$

7.
$$\begin{array}{r} 3 \\ -\ 2.19 \end{array}$$

8.
$$\begin{array}{r} 6 \\ -\ 3.592 \end{array}$$

10.
$$\begin{array}{r} 3 \\ -\ 2.146 \end{array}$$

16.
$$\begin{array}{r} 7 \\ -\ 2.455 \end{array}$$

17.
$$\begin{array}{r} 6 \\ -\ 0.324 \end{array}$$

12.
$$\begin{array}{r} 6 \\ -\ 3.145 \end{array}$$

13.
$$\begin{array}{r} 10 \\ -\ 5.033 \end{array}$$

A Smart Butterfly

When multiplying with decimals, place the decimal point in the product, counting from right to left, the same number of places as the sum of the decimal places in the factors.

$ 6.95   The decimal point is 2 places, $ 6.95   Place the decimal point 2
x   3   counting from right to left, in the   x   3   places, counting from right
          top factor. There is no decimal point $ 20.85 to left, in the product.
          in the bottom factor. 2 + 0 = 2

Multiply. Then, use the code to answer the riddle below.

I
```
    2.8
x    3
```

E
```
   26.5
x    4
```

A
```
   32.8
x    7
```

T
```
  20.41
x    5
```

W
```
   0.24
x    9
```

O
```
   0.04
x    8
```

H
```
   3.06
x    6
```

S
```
  30.01
x    8
```

I
```
  24.81
x    6
```

T
```
   24.6
x    5
```

I
```
   41.5
x    3
```

M
```
  0.416
x     5
```

T
```
   45.6
x    8
```

M
```
   48.5
x    3
```

C
```
   4.53
x    3
```

N
```
   3.08
x    4
```

A
```
   3.49
x    7
```

A
```
   6.94
x    9
```

Why did the butterfly learn decimals?

___ ___   ___ ___ ___   **A**
124.5 123.0   2.16 62.46 240.08

___ ___ ___ ___ — ___ ___ ___ ___ ___ ___ ___ ___ ___ .
2.080 0.32 102.5 18.36   106.0 145.5 24.43 364.8 148.86 13.59 8.4 229.6 12.32

Skywriting, Decimal Style

To multiply decimals, follow these steps.

¹4.6	¹4.6	¹4.6	4.6
x 3.2	x 3.2	x 3.2	x 3.2
92	92	92	92
0	1380	¹1380	1380
		1472	14.72

1. Multiply by the tenth digit. Add a zero.

2. Multiply by the ones digit.

3. Add.

4. Starting from right to left in each factor, count the number of spaces to the decimal point. Place the decimal point in the product.

To discover what the skywriter wrote, shade in each cloud with a product greater than 1.

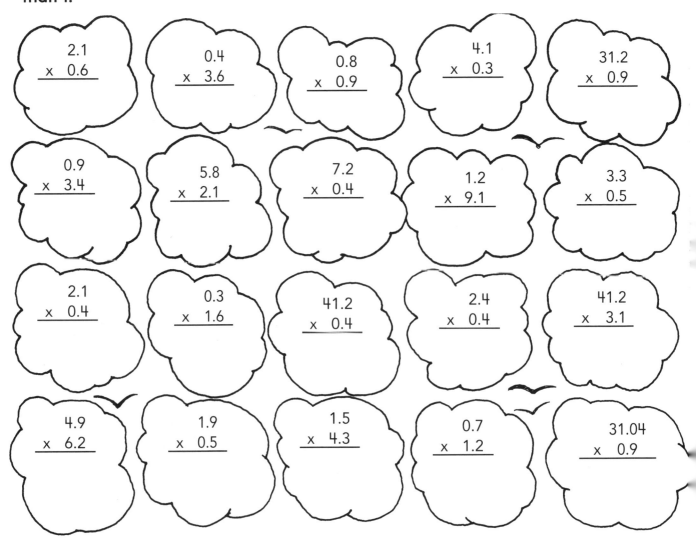

2.1
x 0.6

0.4
x 3.6

0.8
x 0.9

4.1
x 0.3

31.2
x 0.9

0.9
x 3.4

5.8
x 2.1

7.2
x 0.4

1.2
x 9.1

3.3
x 0.5

2.1
x 0.4

0.3
x 1.6

41.2
x 0.4

2.4
x 0.4

41.2
x 3.1

4.9
x 6.2

1.9
x 0.5

1.5
x 4.3

0.7
x 1.2

31.04
x 0.9

Zero, You're Such a Hero!

Zero is such an important number when multiplying decimals. Remember, always place a zero to the left of a decimal point when there are no whole numbers present.

```
    0.004              0.004              0.004              0.004   (3 places)
x     0.6          x     0.6          x     0.6          x     0.6   (1 place)
    0024               0024               0024               0024
       0              00000              00000              00000
                                         00024              0.0024
```

1. Multiply the tenths digit. Add a zero under the first digit to the right.
2. Multiply the ones digit.
3. Add.
4. Place the decimal point in the product.

A million has 6 zeros. To find out how many zeros a septillion has, count the number of zeros to the right of the decimal point in each of the problems.

O O O O O O O O O O O O O O O

```
              0.8          0.09         0.003
          x   0.9      x   0.2      x   0.8
```

```
     0.005         0.01         0.04         0.006
 x   0.3       x   0.7      x   0.03     x   0.6
```

```
   0.3        0.02         13.4         0.02          0.8
x  0.1     x  0.1      x   0.3      x   0.8      x0.009
```

```
   4.9        0.6         21.02        0.13         0.002
x  0.2    x 0.002     x   0.4      x   0.4      x   0.9
```

A septillion has _____ zeros!

O O O O O O O O O O O O O O O O O O

Keep on Climbing

To divide decimals by a whole number, follow these steps.

```
     2                2.4               2.48
  3 )7.44          3 )7.44           3 )7.44
    -6               -6                -6
     1               14                14
                    -12               -12
                      2                24
                                     -24
                                       0
```

**1. Divide the
ones.**

**2. Place the
decimal point in
the quotient.
Divide the tenths.**

**3. Divide the
hundredths.**

If the quotient is less
than one, there must
be a zero to the left of
the decimal point.

0.58 < 1

```
    0.58
 2 )1.16
   -10
    16
   -16
     0
```

**Divide. Then, use the code to fill in the blanks below to complete the fact about
two famous mountain climbers.**

U
4)8.64

L
2)72.8

S
6)9.36

Y
5)32.35

H
5)23.5

R
9)5.22

E
3)267.3

M
2)13.56

D
3)2.67

A
2)1.18

N
3)110.4

I
4)107.2

The first men to climb the top of Mount Everest
were Tenzing Norgay and

___ ___ ___   ___ ___ ___ ___ ___ ___
1.56 26.8 0.58   89.1 0.89 6.78 2.16 36.8 0.89

___ ___ ___ ___ ___ ___ ___.
4.7 26.8 36.4 36.4 0.59 0.58 6.47

Ride the Wave of Decimal Division

Sometimes zeros are needed in the quotient. When dividing decimals by a whole number, follow these steps.

$$\begin{array}{r} 2 \\ 27\,\overline{\smash{)}\,55.08} \\ -54 \\ \hline 1 \end{array}$$

$$\begin{array}{r} 2. \\ 27\,\overline{\smash{)}\,55.08} \\ -54 \\ \hline 1 \end{array}$$

$$\begin{array}{r} 2.0 \\ 27\,\overline{\smash{)}\,55.08} \\ -54 \\ \hline 10\;(<27) \end{array}$$

$$\begin{array}{r} 2.04 \\ 27\,\overline{\smash{)}\,55.08} \\ -54 \\ \hline 108 \\ -108 \\ \hline 0 \end{array}$$

1. Divide the whole number.

2. Place the decimal point in the quotient.

3. Bring down the 0. Since it is still < 27, place a zero in the quotient.

4. Bring down the 8. Divide into 108.

Divide. Then, write the letter for each quotient from least to greatest on the lines below to learn where the 1958 megatsunami occurred.

B $62\,\overline{)\,126.48}$

L $13\,\overline{)\,3.12}$

Y $41\,\overline{)\,102.50}$

A $17\,\overline{)\,51.85}$

A $13\,\overline{)\,62.4}$

K $14\,\overline{)\,84.14}$

I $51\,\overline{)\,18.36}$

S $17\,\overline{)\,86.02}$

A $39\,\overline{)\,81.12}$

U $16\,\overline{)\,11.04}$

T $32\,\overline{)\,18.56}$

L $21\,\overline{)\,64.89}$

A $44\,\overline{)\,46.64}$

Y $51\,\overline{)\,53.856}$

A $31\,\overline{)\,188.17}$

The wave occurred in ___ ___ ___ ___ ___ ___   ___ ___ ___,

___ ___ ___ ___ ___ ___ **. It reached 1,720 feet.**

Lots of Zeros

When dividing decimals, add zeros to the dividend to continue dividing.

$$\begin{array}{r} 0 \\ 5\overline{)4} \end{array} \qquad \begin{array}{r} 0. \\ 5\overline{)4} \end{array} \qquad \begin{array}{r} 0. \\ 5\overline{)4.0} \end{array} \qquad \begin{array}{r} 0.8 \\ 5\overline{)4.0} \\ -4.0 \\ \hline 0 \end{array}$$

1. Does 5 divide into 4? No. Place a zero in the quotient.

2. Place the decimal point in the quotient.

3. Add a zero to the dividend.

4. Divide.

Divide.

1 $5\overline{)16}$ $\qquad$ $4\overline{)23.1}$ $\qquad$ $8\overline{)5.3}$ $\qquad$ $8\overline{)27}$ $\qquad$ $5\overline{)2.8}$

2 $5\overline{)4.1}$ $\qquad$ $8\overline{)14}$ $\qquad$ $4\overline{)7}$ $\qquad$ $5\overline{)29}$ $\qquad$ $4\overline{)8.9}$

3 $4\overline{)31}$ $\qquad$ $2\overline{)6.1}$ $\qquad$ $5\overline{)8}$ $\qquad$ $8\overline{)23}$ $\qquad$ $5\overline{)6.8}$

4 $5\overline{)5.6}$ $\qquad$ $5\overline{)7.4}$ $\qquad$ $4\overline{)3}$ $\qquad$ $8\overline{)45}$ $\qquad$ $8\overline{)2.1}$

 Will completed 4 division problems in 3 minutes. How long did it take him to solve each problem? Show your work on another sheet of paper.

ANSWER KEY

Page 5
2/4, 1/3, 1/2
6/12, 4/8, 5/9, 3/8
1/4, 5/12, 2/6
Extra Activity: 4/9

Page 6
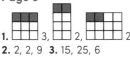
1. 3, 2, 2
2. 2, 2, 9 **3.** 15, 25, 6
4. 24, 4, 10 **5.** 3, 5, 3

Page 7
1. 1/4 = 2/8, 1/3 = 3/9, 2/3 = 12/18,
1/2 = 6/12 **2.** 6, 6, 6, 6 **3.** 30, 10, 12, 21
4. 12, 21, 15, 70

Page 8

Page 9
1. Factors of 5: 1, ⑤; Factors of 15: 1, 3, ⑤,
15 **2.** Factors of 6: 1, 2, 3, ⑥; Factors of
18: 1, 2, 3, ⑥, 9, 18 **3.** Factors of 3: 1, ③;
Factors of 21: 1, ③, 7, 21 **4.** Factors of 7:
1, ⑦; Factors of 8: 1, 2, 4, ⑦, 14, 28
1. ÷ 2 = 2/5, ÷ 6 = 1/2, ÷ 3 = 1/4
2. ÷ 4 = 1/5, ÷ 3 = 1/7 ÷ 5 = 1/3
3. ÷ 7 = 1/3, ÷ 3 = 1/8, ÷ 7 = 1/4

Page 10

Extra Activity: 4/8 = 1/2, 7/21 = 1/3,
2/10 = 1/5, 10/20 = 1/2, 3/15 = 1/5,
6/8 = 3/4, 6/12 = 1/2, 3/6 = 1/2,
6/10 = 3/5, 4/6 = 2/3, 9/18 = 1/2,
10/15 = 2/3, 2/20 = 1/10, 3/21 = 1/7,
5/10 = 1/2, 5/20 = 1/4, 2/6 = 1/3,
15/20 = 3/4, 4/12 = 1/3, 10/12 = 5/6,
4/20 = 1/5, 3/9 = 1/3, 2/8 = 1/4,
8/20 = 2/5, 8/12 = 2/3, 5/30 = 1/6,
4/10 = 2/5

Page 11
1. <, =, >, < **2.** >, >, >, = **3.** >, >, >, >
Extra Activity: They both ate the same
amount.

Page 12
A. 2 4/7 **B.** 4 **C.** 3 4/5 **E.** 3 3/4
H. 2 5/7 **I.** 4 2/3 **K.** 4 1/4 **R.** 7 2/4
S. 2 **T.** 1 3/4 **U.** 3 2/6 **W.** 2 1/5
BECAUSE IT SAW THE TREE BARK!

Page 13

Page 14
**Kids will vote yea and horses neigh
(nay)! They'd rather be munching and
crunching on oats and hay!**

Page 15
1. 5/8, O; 3/4, X; 2/3, O; 3/8, X; 3/10, X;
3/6 = 1/2, X; 6/10 = 3/5, O; 4/15, O;
4/9, X **2.** 7/8, O; 3/12 = 1/4, O; 5/12, X;
6/6 = 1, O; 7/12, O; 5/6, X; 3/14, X;
7/16, X; 7/9, O

Page 16
O. 5/6 **W.** 7/12 **E.** 7/10 **G.** 17/21 **S.** 1 7/15
A. 2/3 **L.** 11/28 **O.** 11/15 **I.** 1 11/20
N. 13/18 **R.** 17/20 **D.** 1 1/6 **H.** 1 9/40
!. 8/15 **U.** 37/56 **N.** 3/4 **Y.** 19/28
HE WAS ALWAYS HORSING AROUND!

Page 17
1. 4 5/8, 7 1/6, 5 1/4 **2.** 3 1/2, 3 2/3, 3 5/6
3. 7 5/6, 5 1/8, 5 2/3, 6 2/3 **4.** 3 17/20,
3 7/9, 9 1/6, 5 1/8

Page 18
A. 1/14 **B.** 2/15 **C.** 1/4 **D.** 7/12 **E.** 1/14
F. 8/25 **G.** 1/4 **H.** 1/10 **I.** 2/9 **J.** 7/12
K. 1/12 **L.** 3/10 **M.** 5/14 **N.** 11/18 **O.** 2/5
Grand Canyon National Park covers
1,218,375 acres.

Page 19
1. 3/10, 5/24, 1/6, 1/12
2. 3/10, 7/15, 5/12, 11/20
3. 17/28, 19/30, 7/18, 1/6
4. 1/35, 1/14, 13/24, 4/15
5. 17/40, 11/21, 7/18, 2/15

Page 20
1. 3 2/5, 1 1/7, 2 1/5
2. 4 1/3, 4 1/2, 2 1/4, 3 3/10, 1 3/11
3. 3 1/2, 3 1/2, 4 1/4, 5 3/7, 2 1/8
4. 6 7/12, 6 1/4, 4 1/9, 5 1/2, 2 1/12

Page 21
**Because you don't owe anything at the
end of the problem!**

Page 22
E. 5 1/2 **I.** 2 1/2 **T.** 1 3/5 **A.** 5 4/7
L. 2 3/4 **W.** 1 2/3 **E.** 4 4/5 **L.** 3 2/5
T. 4 2/3 **C.** 1 2/5 **N.** 1 4/7 **G.** 2 4/5
S. 3 4/7 **M.** 5 5/6 **J.** 7 4/7
The largest meteorite found in the
United States is called the **WILLAMETTE**
meteorite.

Page 23
1. 1 1/5, 2, 1 3/4, 3 1/3 **2.** 2, 1/2, 4, 3
3. 3 3/4, 5/6, 2, 6 **4.** 4 1/5, 3, 1 1/2, 3 1/3
5. 4 2/3, 2/3, 4 1/2, 1 3/4
Extra Activity: 8 x 3/4 = 6 boxes

Page 24
1. 1/9, 2/5, 3/8, 1/12
2. 1/30, 1/4, 1/6, 1/4
3. 1/4, 1/16, 1/50, 1/18
4. 1/5, 1/12, 1/6, 5/12
5. 3/14, 1/20, 1/8, 1/2
6. 3/10, 4/9, 1/18, 3/14

Page 25
1. 3, cowhand; 1 2/7; 1 3/10
2. 7/10, bookworm; 2, boardwalk; 1 2/5
3. 1 5/8; 1/4, housefly; 1 1/7
4. 2, toenail; 2/3, carpool; 4/15, cowboy

Page 26
1. 21, 14, 8, 32, 12 **2.** 15, 9, 27, 6, 8
3. 15, 6, 2, 30, 12 **4.** 16, 18, 10, 20, 12
The diameter of the sun is **865,000**
miles.

Page 27
1. 0.2, 0.5, 0.8, 0.4
2. 0.75, 0.375, 0.6, 0.875
3. 0.2, 0.25, 0.3, 0.25
4. 0.12, 0.5, 0.35, 0.36
5. 0.7, 0.625, 0.9, 0.6

Page 28

Page 29

0.4, I; 0.6, only; 0.2, want; 0.5, one; 0.1, tenth; 0.9, of; 0.7, that; 0.8, cracker; 0.3, in; 5.7, your; 8.3, hand

Page 30

1. 3.54 **2.** 56.72 **3.** 0.98 **4.** 24.02
5. 304.03 **6.** 75.13 **7.** 843.06 **8.** 89.22
9. 131.71 **10.** 0.69 **11.** 52.32 **12.** 400.57
13. 27.04 **14.** 48.03 **15.** 14.62 **16.** 786.02
17. 445.64 **18.** 625.54 **19.** 928.24 **20.** 4.9

Page 31

1. 1.169 **2.** 9,357.1 **3.** 32.006
4. 7.384 **5.** 46.334

Page 32

Across: 1. six tenths **3.** eight hundredths
4. fifty-four thousandths **5.** five tenths
6. three tenths **7.** two hundredths
8. nine hundredths **10.** five hundredths
11. thirty-two hundredths **12.** twenty-six thousandths
Down: 1. seven thousandths **2.** six hundredths **4.** four tenths **9.** two tenths
Check student's crosswords.

Page 33

1. <, >, <, < **2.** >, =, >, < **3.** =, >, >, =
4. >, <, < **5.** >, < **6.** <, > **7.** <, <

Page 34

2. 7.0, 7.3, 7.7, 7.9, **MODE**
3. 0.2, 0.3, 0.5, 0.8, **GRID**
4. 1.9, 3.6, 5.7, 8.4, **AREA**
5. 2.16, 2.47, 2.89, 2.98, **CUBE**
6. 0.59, 3.93, 6.48, 8.42, **FACE**
7. 0.409, 4.09, 6.409, 6.904, **MEAN**
8. 0.92, 3.92, 4.06, 6.9, **LINE**
9. 1.8, 4.84, 5.45, 9.08, **INCH**
10. 1.248, 1.482, 1.824, 1.842, **FLIP**
11. 0.59, 5.09, 9.005, 9.05, **TERM**

Page 35

1. Round down: 2.2 = 2, 3.4 = 3, 4.1 = 4, 5.2 = 5 **Round up:** 2.6 = 3, 2.9 = 3, 3.7 = 4, 4.5 = 5, 4.9 = 5, 5.8 = 6
Round down: 6.1 = 6, 6.4 = 6, 7.2 = 7, 7.4 = 7, 8.2 = 8, 9.1 = 9, 9.3 = 9
Round up: 6.5 = 7, 7.9 = 8, 8.5 = 9, 9.8 = 10
2. Round down: 5.14 = 5.1, 5.23 = 5.2, 5.31 = 5.3, 5.34 = 5.3, 5.44 = 5.4, 5.15 = 5.2, 5.19 = 5.2 **Round up:** 5.28 = 5.3, 5.38 = 5.4, 5.49 = 5.5 **Round down:** 7.42 = 7.4, 7.51 = 7.5, 7.64 = 7.6, 7.72 = 7.7
Round up: 7.45 = 7.5, 7.48 = 7.5, 7.55 = 7.6, 7.69 = 7.7, 7.75 = 7.8, 7.78 = 7.8

Page 36

1. 0.19, 0.62, 0.54, 0.85, 0.65, 0.66, 0.33, 0.91, 0.69, 0.75 **Order:** 0.19, 0.33, 0.54, 0.62, 0.66, 0.69, 0.75, 0.85, 0.91
2. 6.42, 5.91, 4.26, 3.69, 5.35, 4.18, 3.15, 6.55, 7.31, 9.43 **Order:** 3.15, 3.69, 4.18, 4.26, 5.35, 5.91, 6.42, 6.53, 7.31, 9.43

Page 37

1. 3.00 + 2.36 = 5.36, 0.6 + 0.3 = 0.9, 6.4 + 3.8 = 10.2, 1.32 + 3.21 = 4.53, 8.4 + 2.134 = 10.534
2. 3.04 + 2.06 = 5.10, 0.8 + 0.4 = 1.2, 0.7 + 7.4 = 8.1, 0.43 + 3.41 = 3.84, 6.4 + 1.3 = 7.7 **3.** 3.4 + 2.3 = 5.7, 6.14 + 1.23 = 7.37, 2.341 + 0.153 = 2.494, 1.34 + 7.14 = 8.48, 1.312 + 2.416 = 3.728

Page 38

1. 0.203 + 6.2 + 7.06 = 13.463, 1.048 + 34.218 + 3.214 = 38.480, 1.003 + 2.14 + 26.31 = 29.453
2. 21.04 + 0.243 + 0.246 = 21.529, 0.343 + 7.06 + 8.141 = 15.544, 21.04 + 1.048 + 0.246 = 22.334
3. 13.102 + 34.218 + 7.06 = 54.380, 0.343 + 0.246 + 1.003 = 1.592, 21.04 + 0.203 + 26.31 = 47.553
4. 34.218 + 1.003 + 2.14 = 37.361, 8.141 + 1.003 + 0.246 = 9.390, 1.048 + 3.214 + 0.203 = 4.465
5. 0.243 + 21.04 + 7.06 = 28.343, 13.102 + 34.218 + 6.2 = 53.520, 23.142 + 21.04 + 3.214 = 47.396
6. 26.31 + 34.218 + 7.06 = 67.588, 23.142 + 1.048 + 8.141 = 32.331, 0.246 + 21.04 + 3.214 = 24.500, 1.048 + 0.343 + 2.14 = 3.531

Page 39

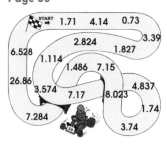

Page 40

Across: 4. 2.998 **5.** 1.018 **6.** 1.533
7. 0.597 **8.** 2.52 **9.** 10.11 **11.** 5.454
14. 3.998 **15.** 9.588 **16.** 4.545 **17.** 5.676
Down: 1. 1.994 **2.** 2.581 **3.** 1.109 **4.** 2.358
6. 1.52 **7.** 0.81 **8.** 2.408 **10.** 0.854
12. 2.855 **13.** 4.967
Check student's crosswords.

Page 41

I. 8.4 **E.** 106.0 **A.** 229.6 **T.** 102.05
W. 2.16 **O.** 0.32 **H.** 18.36 **S.** 240.08
I. 148.86 **T.** 123.0 **I.** 124.5 **M.** 2.080
T. 364.8 **M.** 145.5 **C.** 13.59 **N.** 12.32
A. 24.43 **A.** 62.46
IT WAS A MOTH-EMATICIAN.

Page 42

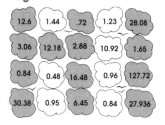

Page 43

0.72, 0.018, 0.0024; 0.0015, 0.007, 0.0012, 0.0036; 0.03, 0.002, 4.02, 0.016, 0.0072; 0.98, 0.0012, 8.408, 0.052, 0.0018
A septillion has **24** zeros!

Page 44

U. 2.16 **L.** 36.4 **S.** 1.56 **Y.** 6.47 **H.** 4.7
R. 0.58 **E.** 89.1 **M.** 6.78 **D.** 0.89
A. 0.59 **N.** 36.8 **I.** 26.8
SIR EDMUND HILLARY

Page 45

B. 2.04 **L.** 0.24 **Y.** 2.5 **A.** 3.05 **A.** 4.8
K. 6.01 **I.** 0.36 **S.** 5.06 **A.** 2.08 **U.** 0.69
T. 0.58 **L.** 3.09 **A.** 1.06 **Y.** 1.056 **A.** 6.07
The wave occurred in **LITUYA BAY, ALASKA**. It reached 1,720 feet.

Page 46

1. 3.2, 5.775, 0.6625, 3.375, 0.56
2. 0.82, 1.75, 1.75, 5.8, 2.225
3. 7.75, 3.05, 1.6, 2.875, 1.36
4. 1.12, 1.48, 0.75, 5.625, 0.2625
Extra Activity: 0.75 minutes